Carried

MOTHERHOOD
| miscarriage

Keleah Brown

DEDICATION

Without my beautiful family, there would be no book.

Part One: Life
Part Two: Loss
Part Three: Longing
Part Four: Love

This book has been my therapy; counseling in written form.

PART ONE:

LIFE

KELEAH BROWN

Disbelief bounces back from the berried stick.
Two eyes stare at two lines.
Two tests, to make sure.
Too soon, I thought.
Tears crowded my eyes as he said,
"It will be alright."
"I love you, what are we going to do?", I ask.
"Prepare".

-the first test

I think of the women who do not have the support and encouragement of their partner. Those women who do not know that things will be alright or who cannot see the route to take. I, blessed, should be grateful.

-thoughts

Standing up from the now-warmed toilet seat, life was different. My knees buckled at the effort to move, my chest tightened at the thought of new life. Life unwrapped and tucked safely away. And tomorrow, joy came. Renewed in mind, I was able to notice the blossoming; a beginning.

-in a good way

Taking pictures of each month's progression, that little belly grows. But, how, can I be sure that nothing is going wrong? Never do I think that anything could be wrong. How could it be? This life was a gift to me and perfect in every way. Not a worry. Not one doubt. Not a fear, nor a shock. A connection that books and magazines couldn't capture. A joy that only experience can offer. It was love; unforced, unconditional, unbelievable. Without a hand to grab, eyes to seek, or cheeks to rub, it was love.

-the first bump

Well, well, well, little baby wants to ball up when it's ultrasound time. "Drink some orange juice", the technician suggested. Instantly, baby bean began squirming around. We'd chosen a name already that would be used for a baby boy or baby girl. Really, I just wanted to not call the little baby "it".

Technician: "Oh my, that's a penis, for sure". Through chuckles, "That's right", said my husband. A tear escaped his ducts, too quick for him to know that I noticed.

-you had to be there.

Walking through a college campus, 8 months of love attached to my frame, awaiting a comment. Sitting in awkward, small, narrow, [did I say small?] desks, pretending to be awake. Determined to not take a semester off, partly because of want, partly because of need, mainly because of judgment.

-two thousand fourteen

I forgot to wear nursing pads one day. Not noticing until my shirt was soaked with eager milk, I stuffed my bra with tissue, and asked a friend for a jacket that I could not zip. This gave my professor one more reason to label me as a stereotype. Sitting in that small, small desk, I began my exam.

-dirty looks

Bath soaks

Back rubs

Ball bounces

Belly holds

Limped walking

& Crushed ice

-in labor

Am I scared? Do I just want it to happen? I can't believe I am about to meet my baby boy, my first born. Actually, I'm not afraid; I'm annoyed. I usually get annoyed when I can't avoid pain and I am anticipating something.

-i inherited that from my mother

In between contractions

feeling every ounce of pain,

I recite Psalms 23

 -*the Lord is my shepherd*

After 17.5 hours of labor,

many unanswered phone calls,

the NFL draft, and fatigue,

our prince decides he has kept us waiting long
enough.

-time to push

My husband, prepared for anything, stood in front of me.

"Alright, let's do this", he whispered, touching my thigh.

Seconds before my first push, a midwife rushes in.

"Push", she instructed from behind my husband.

-first in command

"Don't scream" the midwife whispered; I listened.

-determined

"He has hair", my husband yelled

-i thought he would be bald

Inhale

Push

Grunt

Exhale

Inhale

Push

Grunt

Exhale

-working hard

"He's perfect", I cried.

-*my first born*

My first baby, begging to see the world

wanting to see faces,

waiting

for

milk.

-after birth

Saturday birth

&

Monday classes.

-life doesn't slow down

1. Swollen lady parts

2. Hemorrhoids

3. Constipation

4. Spray bottles full of water

5. Wet wipes

6. Bladder infections

-pain after delivery

1. Baby on one side, pump on the other

2. Soothe my bleeding nipples with lanolin

3. Clean all 1,000 pieces of the breast pump

4. Attempt homework

5. Fall asleep instead

-in that order

Nursing while video chatting with my professor about a Spanish immersion assignment, milk drips on the keyboard. A whine, when he couldn't find the nipple, my professor's puzzled look says it all.

-raising an infant

Struggling to stash

breast milk.

For school.

For work.

For date nights.

For peace of mind.

-it was harder than I thought

PART TWO:

LOSS

Uneducated about trying to conceive, I wanted to get pregnant.
Thinking that all it took was 1 time, and month after month, that proved to be wrong.

I once thought that it only took deciding how many children you wanted and determining the amount of years you wanted in between them.

-life lessons

1. Ovulation strips

2. Mucus testing

3. Period tracking

4. Symptom fixation

5. Herb and vitamin research

6. Blogs, apps, and books

7. Pregnancy testing

8. The start of a new cycle

-overwhelming

"Mommy, I want a brother and a sister"

"When are y'all going to have another baby"

"It's about time, you aren't getting any younger"

"Hurry up, before it's too late"

Cringing with each syllable. Moaning at each inquiry.

-influences

I test, before my missed period.

Finally,

we're pregnant!

Who should we tell first,

And when?

Boiling with excitement, I just want to tell everyone.

-the phone calls begin

"Alright, let's find the heart beat" the midwife told us

nothing

"It's very early, 12 weeks,

 I'm sure everything is okay, don't fret" she reassured us.

My mind, in a million places, focuses on one thing / what if?

-*thick silence*

Trying to remain positive, I scheduled another ultrasound elsewhere. They found a heartbeat. Relief covered me

-thankful

Red stained tissue

during a bathroom break at work

startled me. I texted my husband,

sent a picture too.

-schedule an appointment

"Are you experiencing excruciating pain?", they ask

"No", I answer.

"Okay, we will schedule you two weeks out", they respond

"Can you see me today?", I rebuttal.

-the answer is no

Four days pass, and I call back.

"I am worried".

"Have you had an increase in blood flow since your last call?"

"No".

"Oh, honey, don't worry then; sometimes women bleed. Call us back if you experience pain or an increase in blood flow".

-no help

The morning after my birthday,

clots and heavy blood.

Still, no pain.

My husband drove us to the Emergency Room.

At this moment, I realized you can have a blank mind and deep thoughts at the same time.

-lost in my thoughts

I stare out of the window, not sure how to feel. Parking and walking towards the ER doors, things seem to be more real than ever. As I check in and verbalize, "I'm 16 weeks pregnant and I am having bleeding with clots", tears rush down my face.

-emergency room

Tests, blood draws, an IV, ultrasounds, and zero eye contact.

The Emergency Room had become my worst nightmare.

"No one will look at me so something MUST be wrong".

Sitting in a stale room, my family of three exchange looks, prayers, and hand holds.

-the waiting game

A new face enters the room.

"Mrs. Brown, it does look like a miscarriage. The fetus measures at 9 weeks and there is no heartbeat. You will need to head right over to the OBGYN that we refer to. They will talk to you about the next steps and about your situation in more detail. I'm sorry."

-the world stops

My husband and I speak little through words, almost exclusively through glares, tears, and sighs.

-*mutual agony*

She leaves a stack of paper and pamphlets, all referring to a "Spontaneous Abortion".

From then on out,

Every piece of paperwork, every bill, every handout, each conversation: "Spontaneous Abortion".

Everything is so matter-of-fact leaving no room for sensitivity.

-overkill

"You can try to pass the fetus on your own at home. I must warn you, you will experience pain" the doctor describes.

Newsflash: I was drowning in pain.

"A lot of women have miscarriages. It doesn't mean that you are prone to them or that you did anything wrong", she adds.

-i didn't believe it

The doctor leaves the room and comes back with a bag of suppositories and instructions. These little white pills are supposed to be inserted vaginally every so often, forcing my body complete the miscarriage.

-who have I become?

The doctor spoke so casually. She spoke as if I wasn't in a million pieces on her exam table. As if I wasn't dealing with the definite betrayal of my body. As if I could even process her words.

"Worst case scenario, the miscarriage won't complete and you'll need a procedure called a D&C"

I relied on my husband to remember what she said because I had sunk into myself.

-a one-sided conversation

The bathroom is the worst place. Sitting on the toilet is a life sentence. I have to stare at the evidence of my failings.

pops pill

-round one

Forced contractions, alarmingly heavy bleeding,

outrageous clotting, unmatched nausea, killer
cramps, and profuse sweating.

The heating pad cord wrapped around the bag of
chocolates my husband bought me.

-excruciating pain

Mostly I use it in the dark....so I don't have to see it, so I don't have to deal with it, so I can pretend like that will actually help; sitting on the toilet, crying. Might as well turn the lights on because it doesn't make a difference. I know what is there and I know what my body is doing. As I hit the lights, I shake with terror and smack them back off.

Visual connection to emotional void creates shadows that can't be shaken.

-trauma

I look in the mirror at a flabby stomach, knowing that it was empty. it was like a grave and the body had been dug up. This grave I shall live with for all of my days. Covered in dirt, fertilized with stretch marks, and slathered with cocoa butter.

-another tear shed

"You'll undergo a minor surgery to remove the remaining tissue. Not doing so may lead to infection and is probably the reason that you haven't stopped bleeding"

After suffering through the loss and the savage suppositories, here I am.

A D & C scheduled.

A day to heal.

A new state, empty body, no family, and a weak spirit.

-isolation, again.

Head down, captive by my mental. Eyes up, smiling at my new friend. This shell of me, has become me. Bits of who I am, used to be, and will probably never be again, break off: some vanish, some linger. Who I am now is a compilation of that shattered glass.

-emotions aren't always pretty

PART THREE:

LONGING

1. Swollen gums
2. Tender breasts
3. Dizziness
4. "Go test", my husband says on Saturday morning
5. Positive
6. Weak knees
7. Tears of joy
8. A praying husband

-answered prayers

My husband drops to his knees, eyes release tears that have been held for months. Fluids of gratitude rush to meet his chin. His embrace made me sure that everything would be perfect. His joy made me know how months of prayers could be answered. My family, my love would expand.

"Wait until you're 12 weeks", never mind your excitement.

-our legacy, our purpose.

All the things I tried to do right: no caffeine, eating veggies, drowning in filtered water, not sleeping on my stomach, etc.

-any change in lubrication = paranoia

At work

Blood poured, spilling on my white pants. As I spend my lunch break curled up in a bathroom stall, I manage to call my husband.

Tear soaked files scattered on my desk.

-*waiting for five o'clock*

Immediately after work, I sit in a waiting room, in seats that are more brown that usual. The doctor only speaks when necessary. She reviews the screens, charts, and notes. No, not again; I am disgusted at her words.

-miscarriage confirmed

Chunks of my flesh, in beating form,
snatched before midnight
You. Are. Mine.
Tiny flutters travel from abdomen to heart
moving like many moons,
You. Were. Mine.
"Grieve", everyone spits, "accept it".
Grief only being a portion of what takes place.
You. Are. Still. Mine.
Always, you'll be, pieces of me
Now in heaven.

-waiting

Try to smile when greeted. Okay, maybe that's too fake.
Say you have a headache or are cramping.
Don't say anything at all. Okay, breath. 7 hours and 49 minutes to go.
Mere hours before, I am curled up in bed
Now, I'm at work, pretending to care. Who do I tell? No one?
What's my excuse for my lack of productivity?
Shuffling papers induce papercuts, reminding me of my pain, my babies.

-work flow

Oh no, she's coming. "What's the matter honey"? in a sweet Texan accent drizzled with intuition. My eyes race to fill with tears, and I must beat them to the restroom. I must, or she'll know. How long can I hold it together? How long do I pretend? Seems like I'm sworn to secrecy.

-why am I even here?

They'll know, right?

I wear the despair like a cloak, fitting too loose.

Covered in heartbreak and stepping backwards almost.

-*wearing bereavement*

Not being able to take off work and grieve at
home;
they have a hold on me.
For now,
I spin half swings in an uncomfortable desk chair
focused on how much I feel, and how much
I don't.

-i cry during bathroom breaks

Losing my job for having to take too many days off during my probation period. They knew I would also be gone for weeks after the baby's birth. No, they can never say that. Yes, it is true. But, the life developing inside of me was worth every penny lost, and then some.

-counting down the days

I have my body. Thoughts and emotions, twice over.
Why? it's not the right timing? Then what is?
Did my body forget how to swaddle a life?
Was it birth control? Or is it just me? I need an answer that no one can give.
Those who love me say "you did nothing wrong, you can't blame yourself".
Well, I can, and at this time, I will.

-*what's wrong with me?*

Chocolate, cake, hmm chocolate cake. Sodas, gummy worms, sour gummy worms. No breakfast, lunch, or dinner. I'm punishing my body for torturing me. You will not get any nutrients. You will not thrive since half of you is already broken. The irony: it only makes me feel worse. Maybe that's what I want. How dare I nourish myself when I couldn't do the same for my babies. The nerve of me to sleep throughout the night, knowing that I failed. The shameless audacity of my stomach for growling after 19 hours of no food. Where was this alert when you weren't doing your job? My body is cruel, selfish, and yet, alive.

-selfish indulgence

While talking to my mother-in-law about her great news, her natural response is to ask me what's wrong. Not wanting to bring everyone down, but not knowing how to not bring people down. As she receives her best news of her season, I receive the worst of mine.

-raining on the parade

I am battling to not push everyone away and lean on my support system, instead of shutting down and closing everyone off. I've grown up that way; knowing not to talk about it. Knowing that no one really cares. Knowing to cry alone. Knowing to be careful. Really, really careful.

-change

"At least you know you can get pregnant"
"Don't stress about it"
"In due time it'll happen"
"It's not your fault"
"Don't be so sad"
"Just try again"
"Next time it'll happen for sure"
"At least you already have a family"
"It's okay"

-pain, multiplied

People don't know what to say and think they are helping. Well, do they really think that? Have they truly thought through what they are about to say, or does it not matter enough?

A part of me wants to believe that they are only trying to help and that they are saying what they feel like would support us and offer up encouragement. The other part of me believes that they don't care enough to properly formulate a response or put enough effort into what they are saying to someone who is in a fragile state. THINK about what you say before you say it, and don't be careless.

-shameless

People are only going to "care" for a limited time. That concern morphs into annoyance, and self-absorbency. Nudges of time, telling you to move on, do not register; my clock is broken. Your timeline serves you, and not me. What I need is for you to respect my own timeline.

They will distance themselves from you because you're no fun. Stop calling, texting, and asking. They have a life and maybe they don't know how to respond.

-people

The shower is where I mourn most often. Turning the water up a little too hot, crying under the steam. My body is bare, and screams stories of dark pasts.

Standing. Leaning. Sitting. Then laying.

-this body

Headaches after hours of crying

I *felt* pregnant, throwing up from morning sickness
the day before I started bleeding. I was so grateful for
all the uncomfortableness.

I try to suffocate my disappointment and redirect my
anger.
"God, why did you give me this child if you knew this
was the way it'll end up?" I sit and bite my tongue like
cold pressed berries. Hush, I tell myself.

-go to sleep

As a young child I realized that if you go to sleep after an injury, you won't feel the pain. I applied that to my adult problems, except, this time was different. The pain was sharp enough to pierce me through sleep, seep into my dreams, and trouble my blank. This time, is different. Steady into stasis I see closed eyes, a broken heart, and unmatched pain. I see confused people not understanding why I feel this way. "She should be happy that she has a kid", "She is young; she still has time", they squeal, as if it were a blanket prescription.

Emotions so strong, sleep shatters, and hide.

-i seek

Then, there's this thought, buried in my heart, "What if"?

The doctors could be wrong, maybe my baby is fine but has a dark sense of humor.

My breasts are still tender as I sneak my hand under my blouse. Maybe, my little blessing will be fine after all. Maybe, just maybe. With that wish, blood flows (oozes, squirts, splats) faster than it ever has, in massive spurts: my body's response. Rejecting the thought of hope, my underwear fills. Crying is just as natural as blinking these days, I think, not bothering to pat my face dry as I dart to the ladies room.

-false hope?

One last check, before completing what my body had started.

One more moment to remain hollow, one more minute

of agony and grief. One more missed connection.

Gallops of time pass before the doctor returns, "There is no easy way to say this".

As the screen shows a second sac, tears spill on my exposed stomach.

"You've miscarried one twin, we will do everything we can for the other".

-praise God

Fraternal Twins; one's an angel

Just 4 days later, I'm told that there is still life. The sun peaks from behind the cloud of thunder.

The unexpected ultrasound reveals rays of radiance. Tears flow, a combination of joy and fear.

News lays on my mind like a crisp white sheet hanging out to dry. Wind blows it completely over my face. What. Is. This? Gratitude, absolutely. Fear? Without a doubt.

Lord, please let this baby grow to see my face.

-amen

1. Severe cramping

2. Nonstop bleeding

3. Ruined sheets

4. Heating pads

5. Cysts rupturing simultaneously

6. Showers with the lights out

7. Traumatizing bathroom breaks

-miscarrying naturally

Now, wishing I could take back my initial tears of my first pregnancy. I took for granted the beauty and fragileness of life. How gently you must cherish it, lest it break. My first baby, first born, sitting on my lap, asks, "Mommy, where will the baby sleep?" Through tears I teeth, "With mommy and Daddy. A baby bed, too; that's called a crib." He smiled, pleased with my answer.

-grateful for life left. mourning for life lost.

After a morning full of affirmations, I walk into the glass building. "I am here for an interview", I smile. Sitting across from a panel of 4, glares happen before questions. While making eye contact with the questioner, the others focus on my belly.

They asked questions about being able to lift 25 pounds, my ability to not miss any days during the first 4 months, and if I have a support system to help me with this 'transition'. My bare fingers too swollen to fit my wedding set, my face too disappointed to fully smile.

"We will be in touch", the tight-lipped lady voiced.

-i did not get the job

KELEAH BROWN

PART FOUR:

LOVE

My son crawls into bed to cuddle with

me.

His warm cheek against

mine.

"Don't be sad mommy. I love you".

-*my sweet boy*

1. Take your time; healing is a process

2. Your feelings are valid

3. If you ever want to talk, I am here to listen

4. I've been there

5. I'm so sorry

6. Can I bring dinner, or babysit for you?

7. I love you

-helpful phrases from friends

The wounds won't disappear

or fully heal, but,

in your own time,

you will smile again.

-the healing process

Everyone deals with loss differently. You may talk to others or think to yourself. You may cry for hours or scream internally.

But whatever you do, don't ignore it.

-grief

You are allowed to take care of yourself.

Healing does not mean forgetting.

-eternal memories

Holding your baby,

whether in your womb

or in your arms,

makes you a mother.

Loving that child unconditionally

makes you the best mother.

-motherhood

What a cherished experience it is to have conceived life. That precious baby lives, though not on Earth.

-stay strong

Collapse as many times as you need to,

but make sure to rise after each fall.

-*stand back up*

True friends help you to see the sun after holding you while you create rivers of pain. Mumbling "I love you" while you dive into quick sand, with 1 hand outreaching. Husbands who have blackened knees from praying for you, whose words are weighted gold.

-support systems

So much of life is unexplained. So many questions will go unanswered.

Example: How is it possible to live while holding your breath indefinitely?

-the pain of memories

Don't let anyone belittle your feelings

because they do not understand or

they do not care.

Talk about it as much or

as little as your process requires.

-challenge the stigma

1. You are strong

2. You are capable

3. You are responsible

4. You are worthy

5. You are loved

6. You have a purpose

-keep telling yourself

The pain of grief changes you

and *it* changes over time.

-where you are now is not where you'll be

So many women experience this loss and nothing can prepare you. No one can explain to you the pit of pain you'll be in, or what it will take to rise from it.

-you are not alone

This chapter in life is written, but the story isn't done.

-you have love for an eternity

For all days end with the sky's cry.

-tears of peace and suffering

KELEAH BROWN

ABOUT THE AUTHOR

Keleah Brown is an imperfect mother, maturing wife, and North Carolina native. She shares some of her most personal emotions within the pages of her debut poetry book. This book is a collection of experiences associated with motherhood and child loss through miscarriage. Each page's transparency makes this book more relatable to those who have been in similar situations.